THE LIFE OF JESUS

VOLUME 1

Narrative: H. M. Rasi
Illustration: Heber Pintos

The story of the life of Jesus, based on the narratives written by Matthew, Mark, Luke, and John.

Bible references for each episode appear as footnotes for further reading; they are also listed in the last pages of this volume.

Pacific Press Publishing Association
Boise, Idaho, U.S.A.
Oshawa, Ontario, Canada
Montemorelos, N. L., Mexico

All rights reserved. No part of this publication may be reproduced, stored in a retrieval system, or transmitted, in any form or by any means, electronic, mechanical, photocopying, recording, or otherwise, without the prior permission of the publishers.

Available also in Spanish—*La vida de Jesús*

Copyright © 1984
Pacific Press Publishing Association
Printed in United States of America

Library of Congress Cataloging in Publications Data

Rasi, H. M. (Humberto M.)
  The Life of Jesus

  1. Jesus Christ—Biography. 2. Christian biography—Palestine. 3. Bible stories, English—N. T. Gospels. I. Pintos, Heber. II. Title.
BT301.2.R3413 1984   232.9′01   84-14788
ISBN 0-8163-0573-0 (v. 1)

84 85 86 87 88 89 • 6 5 4 3 2 1

Four men who lived in those days wrote the story of his remarkable life—a life that changed the course of human history. We call their accounts the four gospels.

One of them, a physician-historian named Luke, wrote in his introduction...

After interviewing people who were witnesses of these events and carefully gathering the necessary information, I am writing you an accurate report on the life of Jesus.

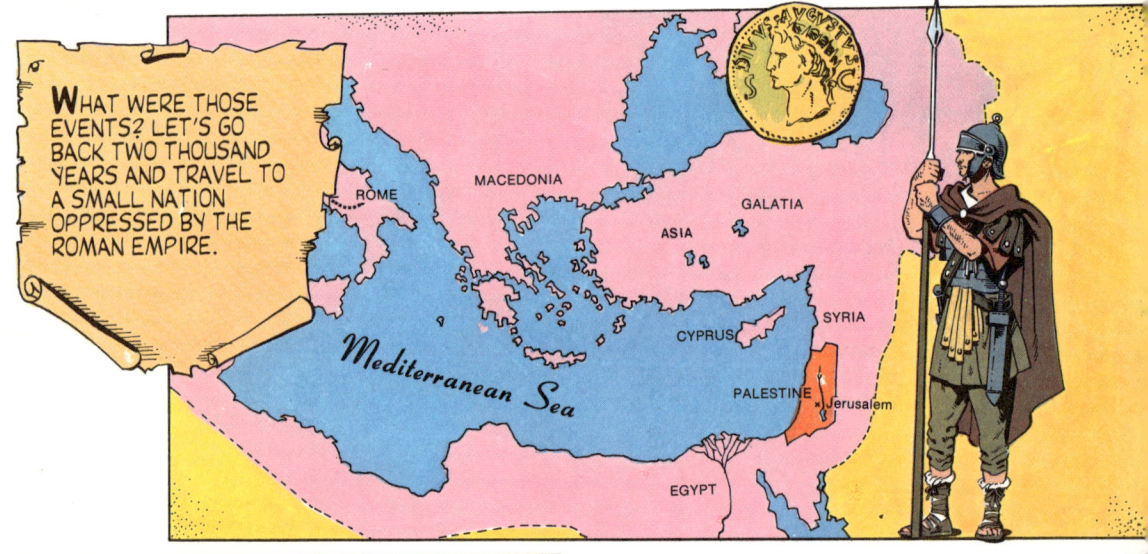

What were those events? Let's go back two thousand years and travel to a small nation oppressed by the Roman Empire.

At the home of Zechariah the priest and his wife Elizabeth...

"I'm leaving for Jerusalem, dear. It's my turn to take part in the temple services."

"Good-bye! Remember to pray that the Lord will give us a child."

"I will, Elizabeth. But you well know how old we are!"

"Yes, but the Lord is powerful, and he can perform miracles!"

2 PROLOGUE TO LUKE'S GOSPEL—LUKE 1:1-4.

3 THE ANNOUNCEMENT TO ZECHARIAH—LUKE 1:5-25.

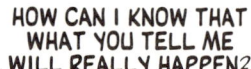

4 THE ANNUNCIATION TO MARY—LUKE 1:26-38.

MARY'S VISIT TO ELIZABETH—LUKE 1:39-56.

BIRTH OF JOHN THE BAPTIST—LUKE 1:57-80.

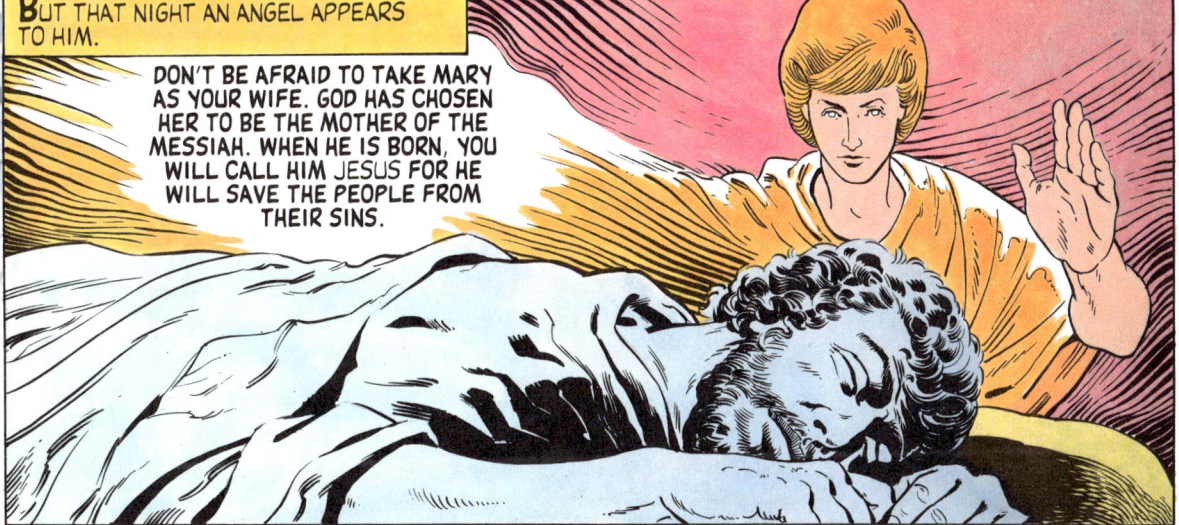

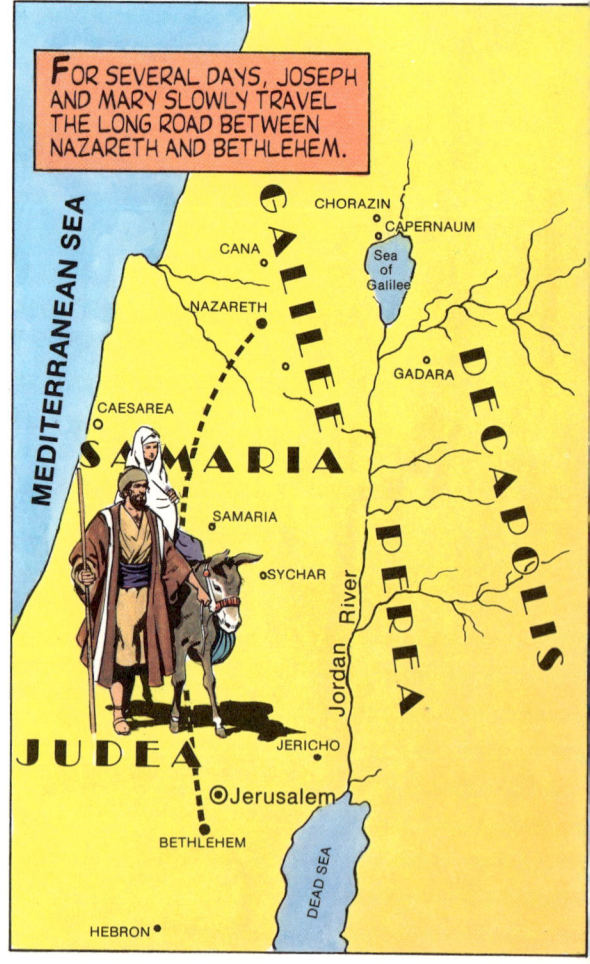

9 BIRTH OF JESUS—LUKE 2:6-7. 10 THE ANNOUNCEMENT TO THE SHEPHERDS—LUKE 2:8-20.

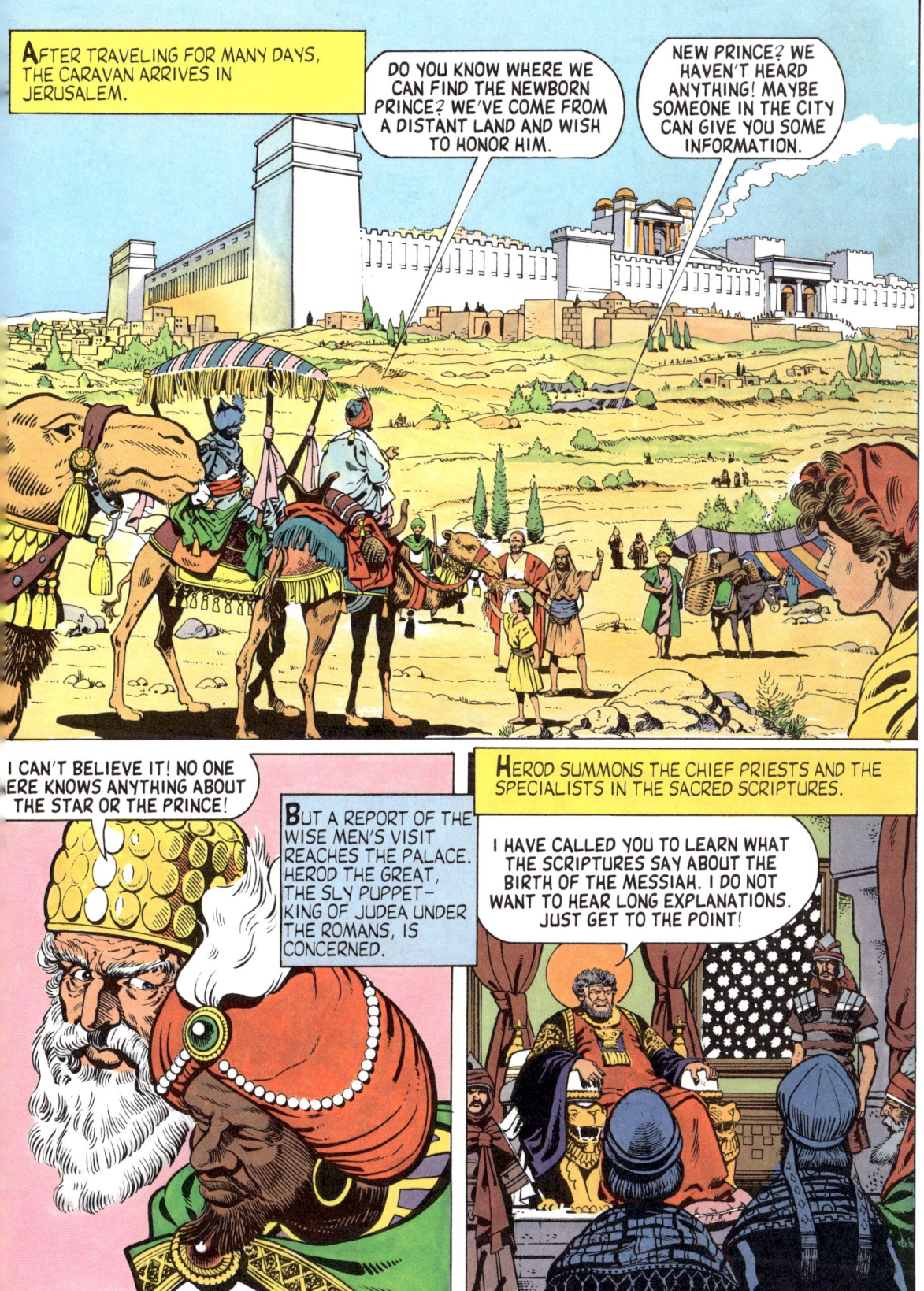

15 RETURN TO NAZARETH; CHILDHOOD OF JESUS—MATTHEW 2:19-23; LUKE 2:39-40.

16 FIRST PASSOVER VISIT TO JERUSALEM—LUKE 2:41-50.

AT THE JORDAN RIVER, JOHN BAPTIZES THOSE WHO HAVE CONFESSED THEIR SINS.

PEOPLE RESPOND TO HIS POWERFUL PREACHING.

WHAT SHOULD WE DO NOW?

THOSE WHO HAVE TWO SHIRTS MUST GIVE ONE TO WHOMEVER HAS NONE. AND THOSE WHO HAVE FOOD MUST SHARE IT.

ALSO AMONG HIS LISTENERS ARE THE DESPISED TAX COLLECTORS, WHO WORK FOR THE ROMAN GOVERNMENT.

TEACHER, WHAT ARE WE TO DO TO ENTER THE KINGDOM?

DON'T COLLECT MORE THAN IS LEGAL.

[20] THE TEMPTATIONS—MATTHEW 4:1-11; MARK 1:12-13; LUKE 4:1-13.

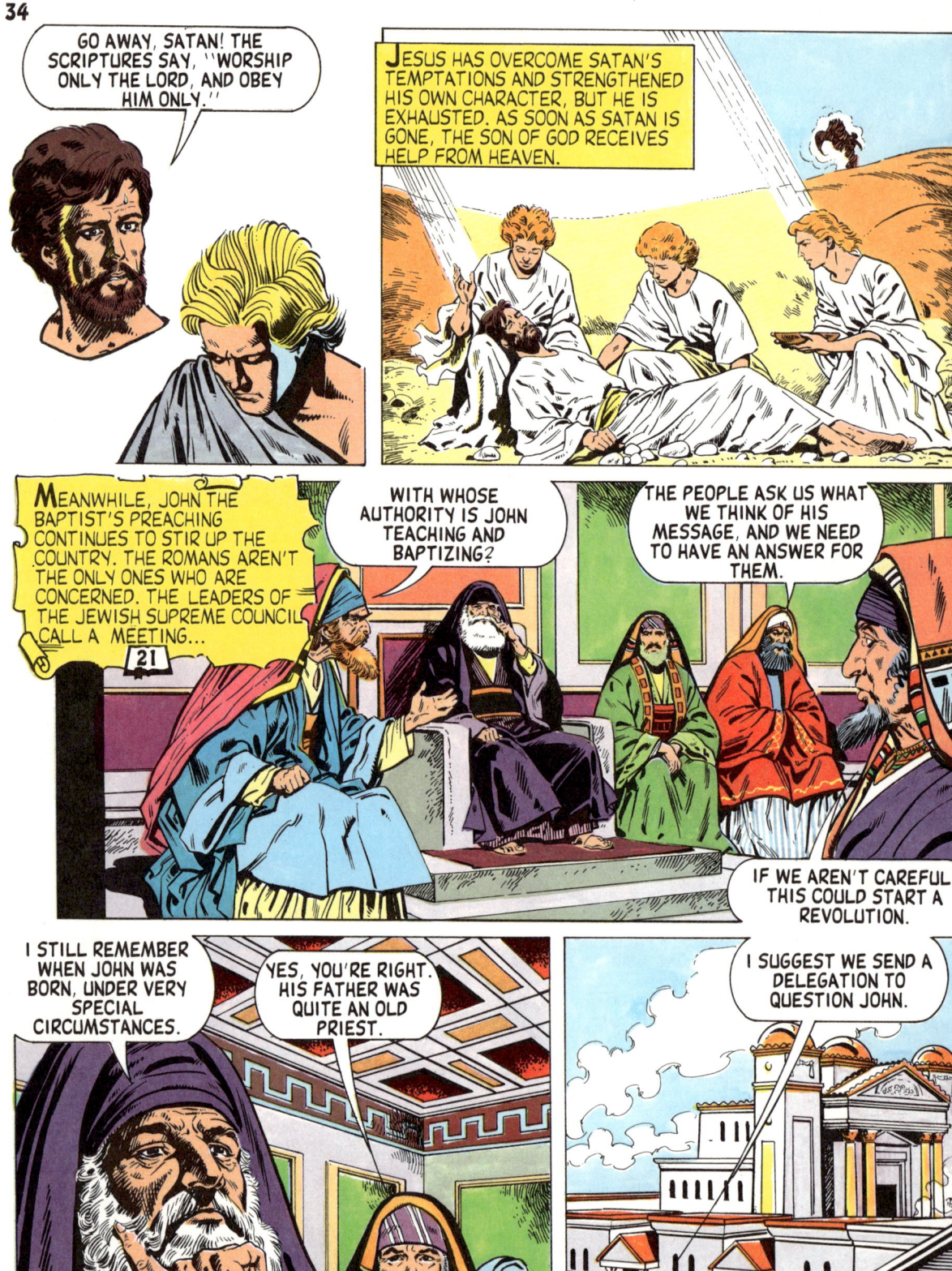

22 THE FIRST DISCIPLES—JOHN 1:35-51.

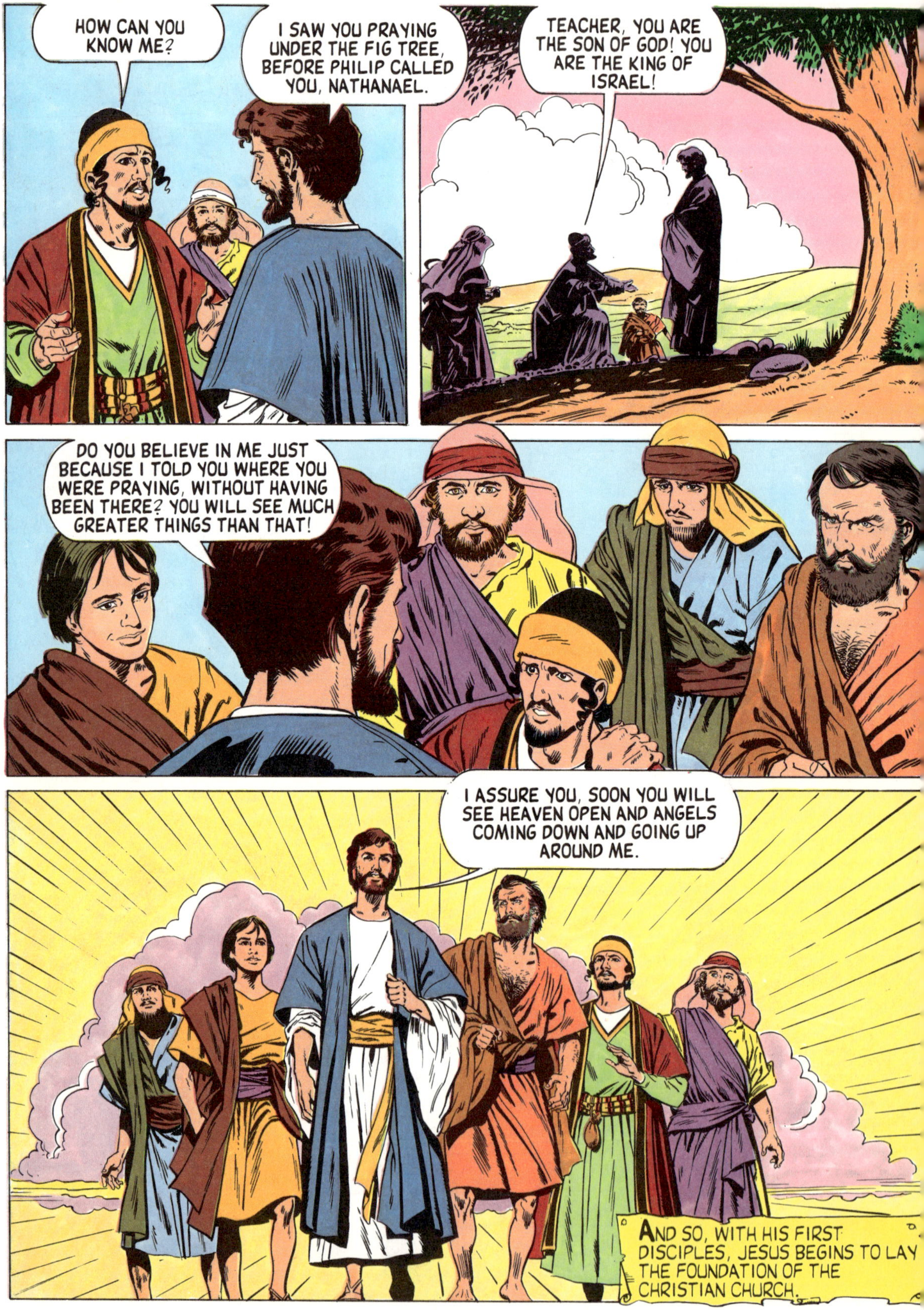

24 FIRST CLEANSING OF THE TEMPLE—JOHN 2:13-25.

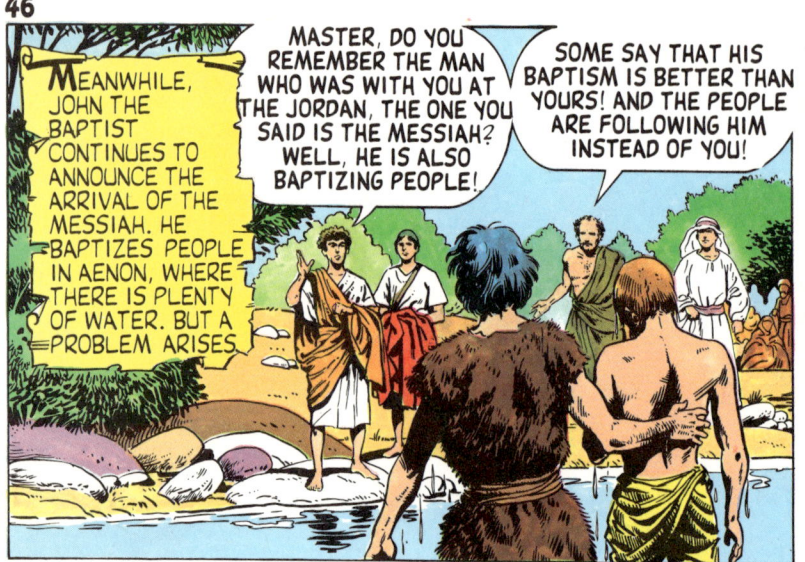

27 THE SAMARITAN WOMAN—JOHN 4:1-42.

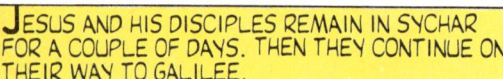

HEALING OF THE SON OF A GOVERNMENT OFFICIAL—JOHN 4:43-54.

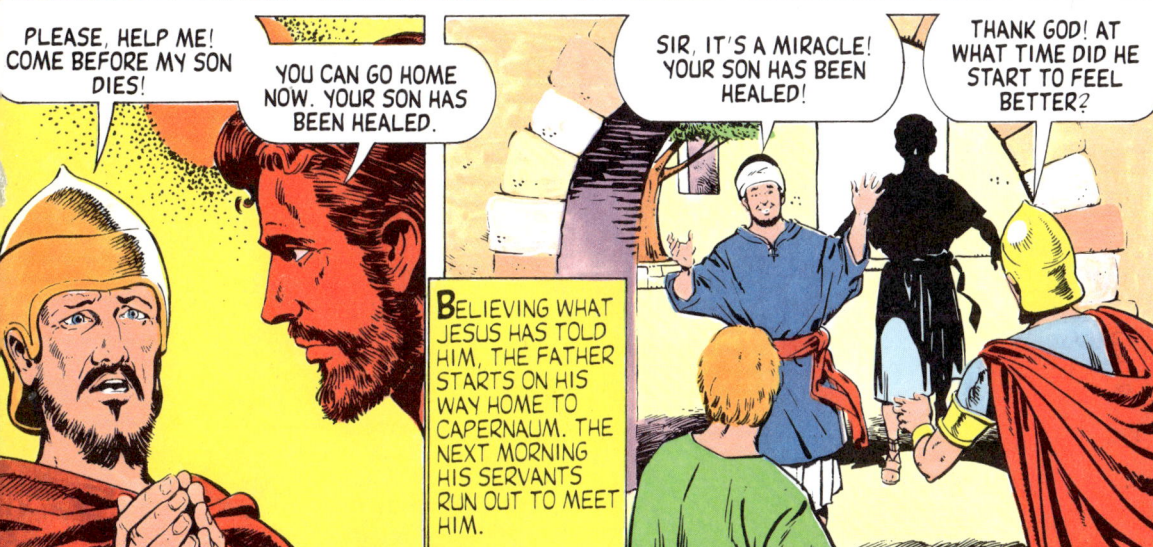

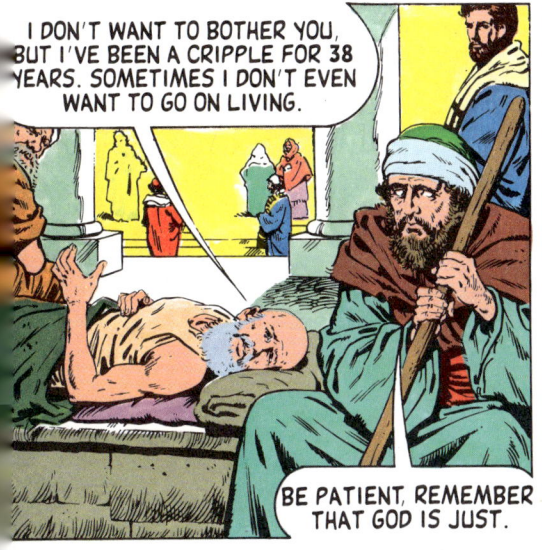

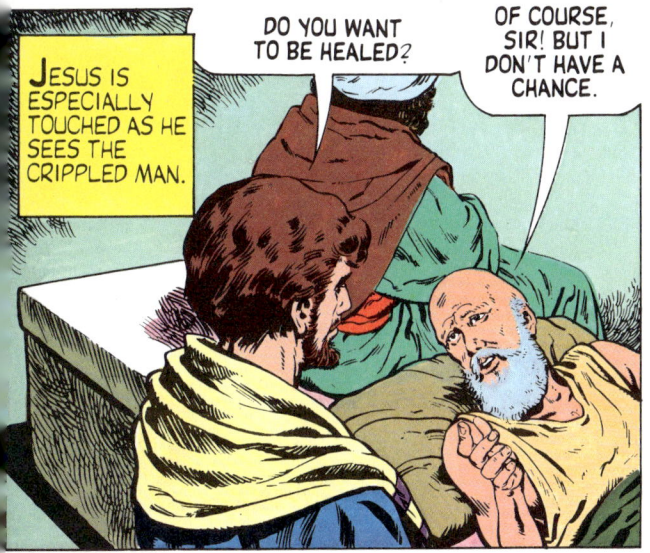

"WE ARE STILL INVESTIGATING THE CAUSE OF THAT STRANGE OCCURRENCE."

"SOON YOU WILL SEE GREATER MIRACLES THAN THIS HEALING. BECAUSE AS THE FATHER HAS THE POWER OF LIFE IN HIM, HE HAS GIVEN THIS POWER TO HIS SON AND HAS ALSO GIVEN HIM THE AUTHORITY TO JUDGE ALL MEN."

"BUT OUR TEACHINGS ARE BASED UPON THE HOLY SCRIPTURES."

"I WISH THAT WERE TRUE! IF ONLY YOU STUDIED THEM SINCERELY, YOU WOULD UNDERSTAND THAT THEY ANNOUNCE MY COMING. AND YET IT SEEMS SO HARD FOR YOU TO BELIEVE THAT I AM THE MESSIAH!"

"WHAT? THE MESSIAH? YOU ARE NO MORE THAN THE SON OF A POOR CARPENTER FROM NAZARETH!"

"WHY IS IT SO HARD FOR YOU TO BELIEVE? I TELL YOU THE TRUTH: HE WHO ACCEPTS MY TEACHINGS AND BELIEVES THAT GOD HAS SENT ME HAS ETERNAL LIFE. HIS SINS HAVE BEEN FORGIVEN, AND HE HAS PASSED FROM DEATH TO LIFE!"

"YOU KNOW THE FATE OF THOSE WHO OPPOSE OUR TEACHINGS AND PRETEND TO BE GOD."

"YES. BUT I'M NOT AFRAID. SOON THE DEAD WILL HEAR THE VOICE OF THE SON OF GOD AND WILL BE RESURRECTED. SOME DAY ALL WHO HAVE DIED WILL RISE AGAIN, ANSWERING TO HIS CALL. THOSE WHO HAVE DONE GOOD WILL LIVE FOREVER, AND THOSE WHO HAVE DONE EVIL WILL BE CONDEMNED. ALL OF YOU STILL HAVE TIME TO CHOOSE YOUR DESTINY!"

"IT'S IMPOSSIBLE TO CONTINUE A DISCUSSION WITH YOU! WE HAVE HAD ENOUGH!"

"GO, BUT THIS IS NOT THE END OF THE MATTER!"

37 HEALING OF PETER'S MOTHER-IN-LAW AND OF MANY OTHERS—MATTHEW 8:14-17; MARK 1:29-34; LUKE 4:38-41.

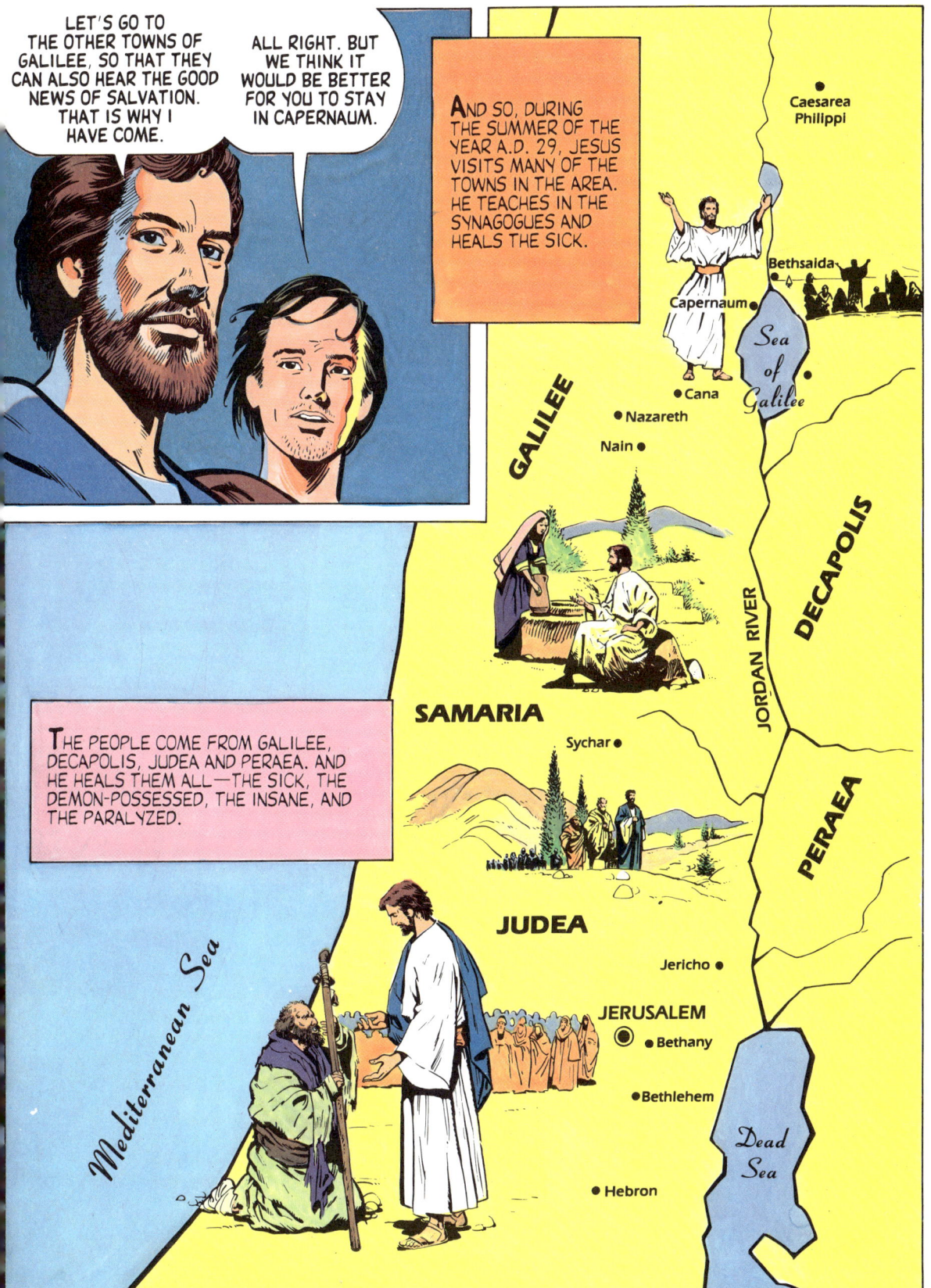

Finally, as evening comes...

45

Tonight I need to be alone, but at sunrise meet me on that mountain. I have something important to tell all of you.

This is a critical moment in Jesus' mission. He is about to choose his closest associates and to deliver his most important sermon. That is why he spends the entire night in prayer, asking his Father to guide him.

As dawn breaks, the disciples walk excitedly to the mountain, anxious to hear what Jesus has to tell them.

From this day on, you will be my special companions. Together we'll share both happy and sad times.

I will tell you about the plan my Father and I have made for the rescue of mankind. Then I will send you out to be my personal representatives, healing the sick and preaching with power.

The Jews believed that the Messiah was going to be a powerful king who would free them from the Roman oppression. And no matter how clearly Jesus spoke, the disciples still thought that he was going to establish an earthly kingdom in Palestine.

As Jesus calls them by name, the disciples come one by one, sobered by the special meaning of the moment.

Some of them have been with the Master for some time, and others have joined the group during these last few weeks.

None of them has been educated in the schools of the rabbis, but Jesus recognizes in them the qualities that will make them strong leaders in the newly organized Christian church.

45 APPOINTMENT OF THE TWELVE DISCIPLES—MARK 3:13-19; LUKE 6:12-16.

THOMAS AND MATTHEW WILL REMAIN CLOSE TO JESUS UNTIL THE END OF HIS MINISTRY.

MATTHEW, WHOSE FIRST NAME IS LEVI, LIVED COMFORTABLY AS A TAX COLLECTOR UNTIL THE MASTER INVITED HIM TO BE HIS DISCIPLE. YEARS LATER HE WILL WRITE AN ACCOUNT OF JESUS' LIFE.

THOMAS, "THE TWIN," IS SLOW IN BELIEVING AND TRUSTING, BUT HE WILL EVENTUALLY BECOME A BRAVE MISSIONARY IN A FAR-AWAY COUNTRY.

JAMES, THE SON OF ALPHAEUS, IS PERHAPS A RELATIVE OF MATTHEW.

NOT MUCH IS KNOWN ABOUT THREE OF THE DISCIPLES—JAMES, THADDAEUS, AND SIMON.

THADDAEUS, ALSO KNOWN AS JUDAS LEBBAEUS, SAYS VERY LITTLE.

SIMON, "THE ZEALOT," IS CONCERNED ABOUT BEING A FAITHFUL SON OF GOD AND A LOYAL PATRIOT.

After Jesus finished choosing the eleven...

"Master, I too am willing to make any sacrifice to become your assistant."

"Accept him, Master. His knowledge and connections will be very useful to us."

Although Jesus knows the heart and destiny of JUDAS ISCARIOT, he receives him as a disciple.

"Father, I present to you these twelve men. Transform them by your Spirit. Give them the power to carry out the mission you have entrusted to me. Guide them daily. Amen."

"THE GATE TO DESTRUCTION IS WIDE, AND A SMOOTH ROAD LEADS TO IT. THAT IS WHY MANY CHOOSE IT. BUT THE DOOR TO ETERNAL LIFE IS NARROW, THE ROAD IS ROUGH, AND ONLY FEW FIND IT."

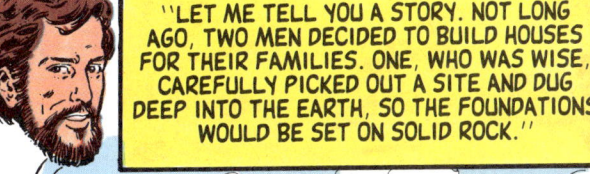

"LET ME TELL YOU A STORY. NOT LONG AGO, TWO MEN DECIDED TO BUILD HOUSES FOR THEIR FAMILIES. ONE, WHO WAS WISE, CAREFULLY PICKED OUT A SITE AND DUG DEEP INTO THE EARTH, SO THE FOUNDATIONS WOULD BE SET ON SOLID ROCK."

"THE OTHER MAN WAS FOOLISH AND DIDN'T STRAIN HIMSELF TO DIG DEEP. INSTEAD, HE BUILT HIS HOUSE ON THE SAND WITHOUT ANY FIRM FOUNDATION."

"LATER, AFTER BOTH FAMILIES HAD MOVED INTO THEIR HOMES, A TERRIBLE STORM CAME. HEAVY RAIN POURED DOWN WHILE THE WINDS HOWLED, AND THE RIVER FLOODED."

"SOON THE HOUSE BUILT ON THE SAND COLLAPSED AND WAS SWEPT AWAY BY THE CURRENT. THE POOR FAMILY OF THE FOOLISH MAN BARELY MANAGED TO ESCAPE."

"WELL THEN, WHOEVER LISTENS TO WHAT I TEACH AND PUTS IT INTO PRACTICE WILL BE LIKE THE WISE MAN, WHO STILL HAS HIS HOME TO ENJOY. BUT THE ONE WHO DOES NOT LISTEN TO MY TEACHINGS IS LIKE THE FOOLISH MAN, WHO LOST EVERYTHING."

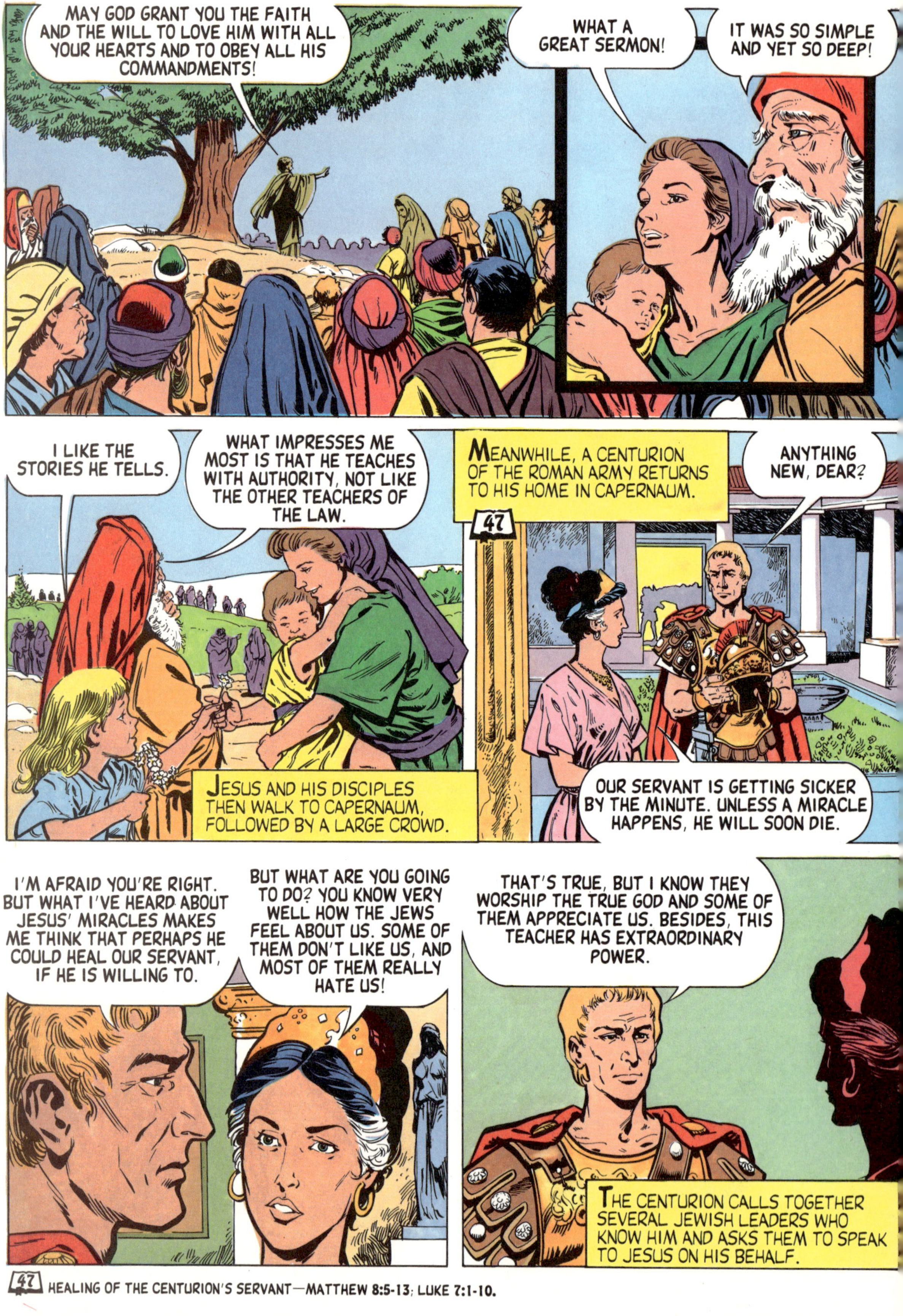

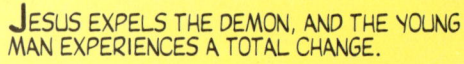

List of Episodes and Bible References

1.	Prologue to John's Gospel—John 1:1-18.	1
2.	Prologue to Luke's Gospel—Luke 1:1-4.	2
3.	The announcement to Zechariah—Luke 1:5-25.	2
4.	The annunciation to Mary—Luke 1:26-38.	4
5.	Mary's visit to Elizabeth—Luke 1:39-56.	5
6.	Birth of John the Baptist—Luke 1:57-80.	6
7.	The announcement to Joseph; his marriage—Matthew 1:18-25.	7
8.	The trip to Bethlehem; the human ancestry of Jesus—Matthew 1:1-17; Luke 2:1-5; 3:23-28.	8
9.	Birth of Jesus—Luke 2:6-7.	9
10.	The announcement to the shepherds—Luke 2:8-20.	9
11.	The circumcision—Luke 2:21.	11
12.	Presentation at the temple—Luke 2:22-38.	11
13.	Visit of the wise men from the east—Matthew 2:1-12.	12
14.	Flight to Egypt—Matthew 2:13-18.	16
15.	Return to Nazareth; childhood of Jesus—Matthew 2:19-23; Luke 2:39-40.	17
16.	First Passover visit to Jerusalem—Luke 2:41-50.	21
17.	Youth and young manhood of Jesus—Luke 2:51-52.	24
18.	John the Baptist begins his ministry—Matthew 3:1-12; Mark 1:1-8; Luke 3:1-18.	28
19.	The baptism—Matthew 3:13-17; Mark 1:9-11; Luke 3:21-23.	31
20.	The temptations—Matthew 4:1-11; Mark 1:12-13; Luke 4:1-13.	32
21.	Jesus declared the "Lamb of God"—John 1:19-34.	34
22.	The first disciples—John 1:35-51.	36
23.	The wedding feast at Cana—John 2:1-12.	39
24.	First cleansing of the temple—John 2:13-25.	41
25.	Discussion with Nicodemus—John 3:1-21.	44
26.	Ministry in Judea—John 3:22-36.	45